WITHDRAWN

PARKER ELEMENTARY SCHOOL LIBRARY

BARRY BONDS

BARRY BONDS

MR. EXCITEMENT

Jeff Savage

Lerner Publications Company • Minneapolis

To Bob Gallicano, the biggest Giants fan I know

Information for this book was obtained from the following sources:
Gentleman's Quarterly, People, San Diego Union-Tribune, San Jose Mercury News, Sport, Sports Illustrated and *The Sporting News.*

This book is available in two editions:
Library binding by Lerner Publications Company
Soft cover by First Avenue Editions
241 First Avenue North, Minneapolis, Minnesota 55401

International Standard Book Number: 0-8225-2889-4 (lib. bdg.)
International Standard Book Number: 0-8225-9748-9 (pbk.)

Copyright © 1997 by Jeff Savage

All rights reserved. International copyright secured. No part of this book may be reproduced or transmitted in any form or by any means, electronic or mechanical, including photocopying and recording, or by any information storage or retrieval system, without permission in writing from Lerner Publications Company, except for the inclusion of brief quotations in an acknowledged review.

LIBRARY OF CONGRESS CATALOGING-IN-PUBLICATION DATA

Savage, Jeff, 1961–
 Barry Bonds : Mr. Excitement / Jeff Savage.
  p. cm. — (The achievers)
 Includes bibliographical references.
 Summary: A biography of the San Francisco Giants outfielder who is a three-time winner of baseball's Most Valuable Player award.
 ISBN 0-8225-2889-4 (hardcover : alk. paper)
 ISBN 0-8225-9748-9 (pbk. : alk. paper)
 1. Bonds, Barry, 1964–   —Juvenile literature. 2. Baseball players — United States—Biography—Juvenile literature. [1. Bonds, Barry, 1964– 2. Baseball players. 3. Afro-Americans—Biography.]
 I. Title. II. Series.
 GV865.B63S38 1996
 796.357'092—dc20
 [B]   96–10081

Manufactured in the United States of America
1 2 3 4 5 6 – JR – 02 01 00 99 98 97

Contents

1

Mr. Excitement

The rain came down hard, and for a while it seemed as though the game at Wrigley Field in Chicago would be canceled. Barry Bonds stood in the clubhouse among his San Francisco Giants teammates. He was swinging a baseball bat back and forth, back and forth, practicing his batting stroke. Barry has one of the best swings in the major leagues, and it didn't come to him by accident. He practices all the time.

The Giants were in first place in the National League West. But with two months left in the 1993 season, the defending league champion Atlanta Braves were gaining ground. The Giants really needed a victory. That is, if there was a game at all.

Then the word came. The sky had softened to a drizzle. The grounds crew rolled the black canvas tarpaulin off the field. They would play. After one inning, though, the Giants wished it had kept raining. The Cubs rocked them for four runs in the first inning.

The Giants fought back. They scored two runs in the third inning and had a runner at second base when Barry stepped to the plate. He was the most feared hitter in baseball because he was leading the league in home runs, runs batted in, and slugging percentage. He could run, throw, field, hit for average, and hit for power—the five things that measure a player's ability.

Cubs pitcher Mike Morgan challenged him anyway. Morgan delivered a fastball. Barry turned on it. *Crack!* The ball sailed high through the soggy air and landed far beyond the rightfield wall for a home run. Barry circled the bases. His teammates greeted him at home plate. His blast had tied the score, 4-4.

"A home run is like a perfect boom," Barry says. "You're in a zone all by yourself. Everything is perfect in that one particular second. It's in slow motion. You don't hear anything, you don't even feel it hit your bat. That's the zone."

Matt Williams was the next Giants batter. *Pow!* Williams conked Morgan's pitch over the fence. Back-to-back homers! The Giants took the lead, 5-4.

San Francisco added another run in the fourth inning to make it 6-4. The Giants were rolling now. The game reached the eighth inning. Then the rain returned. Fans took cover under umbrellas. The game was stopped, and the black tarpaulin was rolled back onto the field.

San Francisco teammate Matt Williams congratulates Barry.

The Giants sat in the visitors' dugout and waited. And waited. And waited. It poured. An hour went by. Their dugout flooded. They had to go back to their clubhouse. Half an hour later, the rain stopped again. The umpire leaned in the doorway. "Let's play," he said.

Cubs pinch hitter Kevin Roberson stunned the Giants in the eighth inning with a two-run homer to tie the game. But with two outs in the top of the ninth, Willie McGee hit a rare homer to give the Giants the lead, 7-6. With two outs in the bottom of the ninth, Mark Grace lined a double to drive in Ryne Sandberg. The Cubs were even again, 7-7. The game went into extra innings.

Neither team scored in the 10th. Cubs ace reliever Randy Myers took the mound the next inning and quickly retired the first two Giants batters. Barry came to the plate. He had to do something. He had to find the zone.

Myers delivered the pitch. It was a low slider. Barry swung. *Crack!* The ball shot skyward. Barry dropped his bat at home plate and watched the ball soar. Centerfielder Sammy Sosa raced to the wall, looked up, and watched the ball fly over the fence for a home run. Barry had done it. The Giants led, 8-7.

The crowd was buzzing over Barry's massive home run when Williams followed with another blast. The ball sailed up, up, up and over the leftfield bleachers. It landed on Waveland Avenue. The Giants had hit back-to-back homers twice in one game!

The Giants won, 9-7. Barry was surrounded by reporters afterward. "It was a good game," he said. "Exciting. Very exciting."

That word also describes Barry Bonds. He's *exciting!*

Barry was an outstanding athlete for Serra High School.

2

Bobby's Boy

Like most young boys, Barry Lamar Bonds dreamed of someday being a professional athlete. Unlike most boys, whose favorite sport changes from season to season, Barry knew all along what sport he wanted to play when he grew up—*baseball.* Barry had the team all figured out, too—the *Giants.*

Barry had good reasons for his choices. His father, Bobby Bonds, was a professional baseball player. The family lived in San Carlos, California, a short drive south of Candlestick Park, where the Giants played.

Bobby was 18 years old when Barry was born on July 24, 1964. A year later, Bobby signed with the Giants organization. Bobby hoped that someday his son would be a major leaguer, also.

Bobby was worried when his baby boy seemed to be lefthanded. Being a lefty would limit the positions Barry could play on a baseball team.

13

PARKER ELEMENTARY SCHOOL LIBRARY

Bobby and Pat Bonds raised their children in California.

Nearly all second basemen, shortstops, and third basemen are righthanded because it's easier for righthanded players to throw to first base. A righthanded player throws the ball across his or her body to first. A lefthanded player must throw the ball away from his or her body to make that throw.

Bobby wanted Barry to be righthanded, and he wouldn't let his son take his baby bottle with his left hand. "I'd pull it away and get him to take it with his right," Bobby said. "But then he'd just switch it over." Barry was a lefty, and that was that. Bobby would just have to help Barry be the best lefthanded player he could be.

Bobby Bonds was an outstanding player for the Giants.

When Barry was two, he could hit a whiffle ball hard enough to break a window. When he was four, his mother, Pat, would drive him and his younger brother, Ricky, to Candlestick Park where the two boys would play in the Giants' clubhouse while the teams were competing on the field. Barry would go from locker to locker, taking sticks of gum. He would stuff as many as he could in his mouth until he was chewing on a giant wad, just like the pros.

When Barry turned five, he got to wear a miniature Giants uniform and play on the field with his glove. He stood between his father, the Giants' rightfielder, and centerfielder Willie Mays during batting practice and shagged flies with them. Mays was one of the greatest baseball players ever. He played centerfield for the Giants most of his career. He is among the all-time leaders in runs, hits, runs batted in, and home runs. To Barry, though, Mays was just part of the family. Willie Mays is Barry's godfather.

Bobby Bonds was a great player as well. He combined power and speed to hit 30 home runs and steal 30 bases in the same season *five times*—more times than anyone in the history of the game.

At home, Barry would play pool with his father in the den. The winner would get to eat his favorite candy bar and watch the loser do push-ups. But Bobby was on the road a lot, and Barry resented it. "I really remember more about my mom," Barry says.

Willie Mays hit 660 home runs during his career. He was also a terrific outfielder and is in the baseball Hall of Fame.

"She did everything for me. She always took me to baseball or football practice. She always wrote 'from Dad' on the Christmas presents. My mom was at all the school events. My dad never went. He was playing baseball."

When Barry's father was home, he sometimes would take his son fishing on a boat in the Pacific Ocean. "I hated it," Barry says. "The minute we'd get out there, I'd get seasick. We never caught anything, and my dad would sit there and eat Oreo cookies. It was gross."

Barry seemed to prefer spending time with his mother. "I was a mama's boy. I'd rather watch my mom put on her makeup," he says, "or I would put on a wig and dance with her. We would both pretend we were Janet Jackson."

Having a superstar for a father was difficult for Barry. His baseball teammates would call him "Bobby" when he got a hit and say he was a good player only because of his father. They were jealous, of course, but Barry's feelings were hurt. He talked about it often with Dave Stephens, his baseball coach at Serra High School. Coach Stephens would comfort Barry.

If Barry was hurting inside during a game, he never showed it. Playing centerfield most of the time, Barry batted .467 in high school and led Serra High School to the Central Coast Section championship round three straight years.

Barry was an excellent baseball player at Serra High School, but he wasn't popular with his teammates.

Barry, No. 34, also played basketball and football for his high school.

Barry also played running back on the football team, and he was an all-league guard in basketball. But baseball was his first love.

Being a local hero was not easy for Barry's father. He would go to many of Barry's baseball games, but he wouldn't sit in the stands. He didn't want to steal the crowd's attention or put extra pressure on Barry. "I'd park behind some trees," Bobby remembers.

From the dugout, Barry would scan the bleachers for his father. Then he would hang his head. "My dad," Barry would whisper, "didn't come to the game." Barry never knew that his father was peering from behind a grove of trees, watching him whack the ball all over the lot.

The Serra High School baseball team was very successful with Barry as a member. He is in the back row, the fourth from the left side.

Barry played three years of college baseball for the Arizona State University Sun Devils.

3

On to the Big Leagues

Barry had always planned to go to college. Then the Giants drafted him fresh out of high school in the second round of the 1982 draft. They offered him $75,000 to sign a contract with them. Barry had a difficult decision to make. He asked his father for advice. Bobby told him to ask for $5,000 more from the Giants. Barry did. The Giants refused. Barry chose college.

Living in Tempe, Arizona, where he attended Arizona State University, was a big change for Barry. It was nothing like living in Northern California. The desert was hot and dry, and there wasn't an ocean or a beach to visit. The Arizona State baseball program was considered tops in the country, but sometimes that wasn't enough. Barry missed his home and family.

The baseball field was the one place Barry felt comfortable. Barry felt safe and sure of himself between the white lines that marked the area in play.

Arizona State baseball coach Jim Brock helped Barry.

Barry played centerfield and felt comfortable there.

Jim Brock coached the Arizona State baseball team. On the field, coach Brock said, "Barry was a kid with a twinkle in his eye." Off the field, though, Barry had problems. He was moody, and some teammates even thought he was arrogant. "I had to talk to him a lot," coach Brock said. "He wanted to be liked. He tried so hard to have people like him. Tried *too* hard. He was never malicious, but he said silly things, wild statements." Barry tried to impress people so they would like him. His boasting often backfired. Some teammates ignored Barry, almost pretending he wasn't on the team.

Again, if Barry's feelings were hurt, he never showed it on the field. Playing in the College World Series as a sophomore, Barry tied an NCAA record by banging out seven straight hits as his Sun Devils nearly won the title. Barry didn't see his family much in college, but he made the most of his time there. He spent countless hours perfecting his baseball skills.

Barry understood that there was more to baseball than singles. He wanted to be a multidimensional player. The Oakland A's spring training site was nearby. A's basestealing superstar Rickey Henderson, who knew Barry's father, worked with Barry on baserunning techniques. Sun Devils batting coach Jeff Pentland taught Barry to use his strength at the plate to hit with more power. Barry responded by clubbing

23 home runs during his junior year. After that, Barry decided he was ready for pro baseball. He declared himself eligible for the 1985 major league draft.

Barry was the sixth player picked in the draft. He was chosen by the Pittsburgh Pirates. As a boy, Barry had watched Roberto Clemente, Willie Stargell, Dave Parker, and other Pirates smash baseballs out of the park. Maybe *he* would be the next Pirate bomber.

First, Barry would have to prove himself in the minor leagues. Each major league team has at least four minor league teams. The minor leagues are divided into Class AAA (the highest level), Class AA, Class A, and the rookie league. Pittsburgh sent Barry to Prince William, Virginia, to play on its team in the Class A Carolina League. There, he met another young player with plenty of potential—a big kid named Bobby Bonilla.

Barry didn't know it at the time, but he and Bonilla would become friends for life. They would hang out together, go to the movies, and share secrets. They shared something else, too. They were both on the fast track to the big leagues. They respected each other, and they teased each other, too.

One night, after Barry had struck out for the third straight time, Bonilla got all the players to throw their baseball caps on the field to honor Barry's "hat trick." Barry was angry at himself for striking out three times when he turned to go back to the dugout.

Bobby Bonilla met Barry when they both played for Pittsburgh's Class A team. Later, they were teammates on the major league Pirates.

Then he saw all the hats, and he burst out laughing. In 71 games at Prince William, he hit .299 with 13 homers and 15 stolen bases.

Barry moved up to Class AAA Hawaii for the 1986 season. But he didn't stay there long. During batting practice, before a game in Phoenix, Pirates general manager Syd Thrift saw Barry hit six balls in a row over the rightfield fence. Barry displayed great power as a pull hitter. (A lefthanded batter *pulls* the ball to rightfield.) The general manager approached Barry and said, "Any good hitter can do that. I'd like to see you hit a few over the *leftfield* fence." Thrift knew that hitting with power to the opposite field is a sign of true strength. Barry whacked five in a row over the fence in left. "Is that good enough for you?" Barry said. "That's fine," Thrift answered. Barry was taken out of the game in the fifth inning, and the general manager took him to Pittsburgh that night.

The next day, Barry was in a Pittsburgh Pirates uniform. He wore number 7 in his first year, but then he switched to number 24 because that's the number Willie Mays had worn.

In Barry's first major league game, the Los Angeles Dodgers arrived at Three Rivers Stadium to face the Pirates. Before the game, Barry checked the lineup card taped to the dugout wall. On it, he saw "Bonds CF." Barry would play centerfield and bat seventh in the lineup. He was thrilled.

Pirates general manager Syd Thrift gave Barry a chance to play in the big leagues.

That night would become even more thrilling for Barry. Against Dodgers pitcher Rick Honeycutt, Barry got his first major league hit—a double, to leftfield, the opposite field.

Five days later, while playing Atlanta, Barry hammered his first big-league home run. The New York Mets were the next team to visit Three Rivers Stadium. Slugger Darryl Strawberry stepped into the batter's box for his first at bat. At first, Strawberry didn't notice anything unusual. The Pirates appeared to be in their usual defensive alignment, with the left-fielder and rightfielder playing deep. But wait—who was the new centerfielder? And why was he standing closer to second base than the fence? Why was he playing so shallow? Nobody plays Darryl Strawberry that close. But Barry caught Darryl's blooper to center.

Barry quickly rose to the majors, but winning came later.

All Darryl could do was yell at the newcomer as he approached second base.

Afterward, Barry explained to reporters what he was doing. "I play a shallow centerfield because I believe if it stays in the park, I can run it down," Barry said. "I know there's a lot of times a Strawberry or an Eric Davis is up, and they're thinking, 'How can he play me there? Move back.' But I'm saying under my breath, 'You can't hit a ball over my head. If you think you can, prove it to me.' "

Who was this brash young rookie named Barry Bonds? Fans were quickly finding out. Even though Barry had missed the first two months of the season, he still ended up with 72 runs, 92 hits, 26 doubles, 16 homers, 48 runs batted in, and 36 stolen bases. He led all rookies in homers, RBIs and stolen bases.

Still, the Pirates finished in last place in the National League East Division. "We are not losers," Barry declared. "We may have lost, but we are not losers. We're young. We're getting better. In a year, two years, somewhere down the line, we are going to tip the city of Pittsburgh right on its ear."

Barry was asked by reporters about his performance. "I'm 22 years old and still trying to find out the type of player I am going to be in this game," he said. "But I'm not so concerned about my own individual self as I am about my team winning."

That was about to happen.

4

Never Quite Enough

Barry had reached the big leagues fast. He could hardly believe he was a pro when he showed up for spring training to start his second year. Here he was, playing against boyhood heroes like Ozzie Smith, Dave Winfield, and Mike Schmidt.

Barry was absolutely in awe the day he faced all-time great pitcher Nolan Ryan. Barry was so over-whelmed he struck out three times in a row, on three pitches every time. One-two-three. One-two-three. One-two-three. Bobby Bonds had told his son to just relax and pretend he was playing in high school. "Are you kidding?" Barry said. "This is Nolan Ryan!"

Still, Barry certainly was focused in the regular season. When the Pirates acquired centerfielder Andy Van Slyke a month into the season, Barry was switched to leftfield. He batted leadoff, scored 99 runs, stole 32 bases, and clubbed 25 home runs. It was a great season.

Bobby Bonds' excellent major league career was hard for Barry to match.

To some, however, Barry hadn't done enough. Barry's father had his first 30-30 season (at least 30 home runs and 30 stolen bases) in his second year. People wondered why Barry couldn't do what his father did. Bobby had retired from baseball the year Barry went to college.

Barry didn't like being compared to his father, but he would only say, "I don't have his strength." Pirates general manager Syd Thrift was more direct. "I'm sure at times," Thrift said, "he wishes he had a different last name." Bobby kept quiet about the issue, not wishing to upset his son. Besides, there was little he could say.

The 1988 season was even better. The fall before, Barry had met a young Swedish woman. Barry and Sun, short for Susann, fell in love and were married on February 6, 1988.

When the season began, Barry was ready to play. In Pittsburgh's first 12 games, he had seven doubles, two triples, five homers, and a .365 batting average. Halfway through the year, he was leading the league in runs scored and home runs when manager Jim Leyland gave him a day off. Barry had a sore knee, and he was pleased to get a day of rest. He was on the bench in the eighth inning with the Pirates and Giants locked in a 3-3 tie. Suddenly, Barry was summoned as a pinch hitter. He unwrapped a bandage from around his sore knee, walked to the plate, and smacked Joe Price's first pitch over the centerfield wall to win the game.

Barry's biggest thrill came late in the season against Philadelphia. First, he watched his father play in an old-timers game and conk a home run. Then Barry rapped out four hits, including a home run, to lead the Pirates to a 10-4 victory over the Phillies. "Having my father there is an inspiration to me," Barry said, smiling. "Maybe I should have him travel with me."

But the Pirates missed the playoffs—again. Barry couldn't get used to losing. Unfortunately, the losing continued the following season.

In one 1989 game at Philadelphia, Barry batted first and drilled a home run. The Pirates scored 10 runs in the first inning. But, in an example of the way the 1989 season went, Pittsburgh lost the game. Barry's homer tied a major league record for most home runs in careers by a father-son combination. But what good were personal achievements, Barry wondered, if the team wasn't winning?

Barry broke the father-son record a few weeks later when he socked a pinch-hit, three-run homer off San Francisco pitcher Steve Bedrosian. The record had been 407 combined homers, held by Yogi and Dale Berra and by Gus and Buddy Bell.

Still, the Pirates wound up being the only team in their division not to make the playoffs during the decade of the '80s. Barry was extremely frustrated. He expected more from his friend Bobby Bonilla and the rest of his teammates. Beyond that, he expected more out of himself.

Then, all at once, the fortunes of Barry Bonds and the Pittsburgh Pirates changed. It happened in a barbershop. Barry explains it this way: "I went to get a haircut. This was in the off-season, in 1989, at Fred Tate's barbershop in Pittsburgh. I'm getting my hair cut, and they have the radio on.

Losing left Barry frustrated and disappointed.

"A guy on the radio says what a great athlete Randall Cunningham is, but what a great *quarterback* Joe Montana is. I weighed the two and thought, I'm so bored with having great *ability*. I want to be a great *player* like Joe Montana. So that haircut was my inspiration. I realized that what I'd been doing—cutting myself short—was wrong. Wrong to me, my team, and even the game. That's when I thought, I'm going to work my tail end off before it becomes too late."

Barry hit the weights. He jogged. He spent hours at a time in the batting cage. He trained alone five days a week, five hours a day. "We'd start working out at 10:30 in the morning," Pirates strength coach Warren Sipp said. "Every day, Barry would be in the parking lot, waiting for me."

Barry showed up for the 1990 season a changed man. He wore a gold-studded earring in his left ear and two-tone "Say No To Drugs" wristbands. He displayed a showy quick-wristed snap catch in leftfield, flicking down his glove when he snared the ball. He moved to fifth in the batting order to drive in more runs. And he clobbered the ball like never before.

The season didn't start out very well. Barry had decided that he would get at least one hit in every game. When he didn't get a hit in the second game of the season, he was furious. "I was mad the whole week," he said. "The *whole week*. I was mad because I blew my streak."

Barry didn't let his anger disrupt his concentration at the plate. He jumped out to a hot streak and stayed hot all summer. He became the talk of Pittsburgh.

"When it comes to ability, Barry's the greatest player I've ever played with, or will ever play with," centerfielder Andy Van Slyke said. "I think one day he will put up numbers that no one can believe," rightfielder R.J. Reynolds said. "He's what this franchise was waiting for," third baseman Bobby Bonilla said.

Barry was polite to his teammates, but he didn't care much for reporters. Sometimes he told them so. Reporters wrote that Barry was "a bad guy to have in the clubhouse." Whispers circulated about Barry's arrogant attitude.

Barry's agent, Rod Wright, defended Barry by saying, "Barry puts up a front because he doesn't want people to know who he is." Manager Leyland also came to Barry's defense, saying, "Barry Bonds plays hard, and he plays hurt. I'm satisfied."

Barry was a terror at the plate. He batted .301 that year with 33 home runs, 114 RBIs and 52 stolen bases. He won a Gold Glove award for his fielding.

Pittsburgh manager Jim Leyland supported Barry and defended him when others were critical of his effort.

Baseball writers selected him as the National League Most Valuable Player. "I'm shocked," Barry said. "My rapport with reporters isn't good." Best of all, the Pirates finally made the playoffs.

In the National League Championship Series against the Cincinnati Reds, the heart of the Pittsburgh lineup fell into a slump. Van Slyke, Bonilla, and Bonds, the three-four-five hitters, batted just .190

with five RBIs in six games. The Reds beat the Pirates and advanced to the World Series, where they swept the Oakland A's to win the title.

Barry's hard work had turned the Pirates into contenders. He led them to another division title in 1991. But again, his bat fell silent in the playoffs. Pittsburgh led the Atlanta Braves three games to two in the National League Championship Series. The Pirates needed just one more victory to reach the World Series. But they lost Game 6 and Game 7 at Three Rivers, and the Braves advanced to the championship. Barry hit just .148 without an RBI in the seven games. Atlanta third baseman Terry Pendleton edged Barry in the league MVP voting.

Then Barry heard the worst news of all. Barry's best friend, Bobby Bonilla, left the Pirates to sign with the New York Mets. Barry cried for days. Then he thought maybe it was time for him to go, too. He had one year left on his contract. Then he would become a free agent and could receive offers from any club that wanted him. Every team wanted Barry. He knew for sure that the 1992 season would be his last with Pittsburgh when team officials told him at spring training, "You're just too expensive for us."

Still, Barry was happy at home. Sun had given birth to a baby boy. Barry and Sun named him Nikolai.

Barry stayed focused on the baseball field. He batted .311 with 34 home runs. He had 39 stolen bases.

New York Mets general manager Al Harazin, left, Bobby Bonilla, and Mets manager Jeff Torborg celebrate Bonilla's joining the Mets with Bonilla's three-year-old daughter.

He won another Gold Glove and league Most Valuable Player award. He appeared as a guest on television programs like *Late Night with David Letterman* and *The Tonight Show.* He was simply the best player in baseball.

For the third straight year, Barry led the Pirates to the playoffs. Once again, though, disaster struck for the Pirates. It was as if Barry's team were cursed in the playoffs. The Pirates led the Atlanta Braves, 2-0, in the ninth inning of the decisive seventh game. Pittsburgh was one inning away from making it to the 1992 World Series. Thousands of fans at Atlanta-Fulton County Stadium stood with their fingers crossed. Millions of people were watching on television.

Barry and Andy Van Slyke, right, were two of Pittsburgh's top players in the 1992 playoffs.

The Braves rallied. They scored a run. The bases were loaded with two outs. The Pirates still led, 2-1. A little-known player, Francisco Cabrera, was sent in to pinch hit. Barry stood anxiously in leftfield. One more out was all the Pirates needed. *One more out.*

Barry imagined a strikeout and then rushing in to celebrate with his teammates. It didn't happen. Cabrera lined a single to left. Barry moved to his right and charged the ball. Dave Justice scored for the Braves to tie the game, and Sid Bream was rounding third with the winning run. Barry gloved the ball quickly and threw hard to the plate. Catcher Mike LaValliere snared the perfect throw. Bream slid. LaValliere tagged him. Umpire Randy Marsh made the call. *Safe!*

Jubilant Atlanta fans poured onto the field. The Braves mobbed Bream at home plate. Barry slumped to the ground and sat motionless. He was stunned. Just like that, it was over. His season—his *career*—with the Pirates was over.

Willie Mays, left, Bobby Bonds, center, and Barry were re-
united in 1993 when Barry joined the Giants.

5

A Giant Star

After leaving Pittsburgh, Barry wanted to play for a team in California. There were five—the San Diego Padres, the Los Angeles Dodgers, the California Angels, the Oakland A's, and the Giants. Barry told reporters, "I want to play for any California team except the Giants because it's cold in San Francisco and they need a new stadium." Barry's childhood dream of playing for the Giants had been replaced by a dose of reality. Candlestick Park was well known for chilly winds blowing off the San Francisco Bay, even in the summer. Outfielders had a difficult time trying to catch windblown balls. It was not a fun place to play.

New Giants owner Peter Magowan called Barry anyway. He said Barry belonged in San Francisco and that he would pay him a lot of money to join the team. He didn't say how much, just a lot of money. Barry thought about the money, about his father, about shagging flies in the outfield as a boy, about coming home. He agreed to join the Giants.

A few minutes later, the telephone rang again. It was Barry's agent. "Barry Bonds," his agent said excitedly, "this is your contract." Barry listened to the numbers. His mouth dropped open. His legs wobbled. He almost fell to the floor. "My head blew up like a balloon," Barry said. "I wanted to go to the Empire State Building and jump, since I could fly at that point. Then I got nervous. Scared." A thousand thoughts and feelings flooded through Barry. The deal was this: six years, $44 million. *Forty-four million dollars!*

In 1993, Giants owner Peter Magowan decided to pay Barry the biggest salary in baseball.

50

Sun and Barry celebrate Barry's decision to sign a multi-million dollar contract with the San Francisco Giants.

The Giants held a press conference to introduce their new leftfielder, who was the highest-paid player in all of sports. Barry was asked what it felt like to come home. Emotions gripped him again, and he began to cry as he spoke. "Will Clark, Matt Williams, Robby Thompson, they're all determined to win," he said. "I have never been more excited to play in a city in my entire life than I am now."

51

The Giants had finished 26 games behind in the standings the previous year. But the 1993 season felt like a brand-new start for Bay Area baseball fans. The new manager was Dusty Baker. The new leftfielder was a superstar. The new batting coach was Bobby Bonds. Barry and Bobby came as a package deal. Dusty Baker and Bobby had become friends in Southern California when they went to the same elementary school. Everything seemed perfect for Barry. Barry's wife, Sun, had given birth to their second child. Now they had a daughter, too. They named their little girl Shikari.

Bobby, left, became the San Francisco batting coach when Barry signed with the team.

Bobby and Barry kept working on Barry's swing.

Barry thrilled fans when he took the field for the home opener at Candlestick Park wearing number 25—his father's old number. Then his godfather, Willie Mays, and singer Michael Bolton, a friend of Barry's, met him at home plate. They presented him with the league MVP trophy that he had won the previous season with the Pirates. A large banner with the words "The Bonds Squad" hung over the railing in the leftfield bleachers. The stadium shook in the first inning when Barry was introduced for his first at bat as a San Francisco Giant. It rocked moments later when Barry hit a fastball high over "The Bonds Squad" sign for a home run.

Willie Mays presented Barry with the Most Valuable Player award for his play during the 1992 season.

Barry didn't get the same reception from Pittsburgh fans a week later, when he arrived with the Giants at Three Rivers Stadium. When Barry took the field, fans showered him with boos and buckets of fake dollar bills. Barry reacted the only way he knew how to react. He went 2-for-4 at the plate with a double, a triple, and three runs scored.

Barry hit .431 in April and was named Player of the Month. After he belted two homers in a game against the New York Mets, Mets manager Jeff Torborg declared, "Bonds belongs in a higher league."

Barry was the leading vote-getter for the All-Star Game. In that game, he smacked two doubles against the American League. If only he could play in the World Series, he thought. Then he'd *really* show everyone what he could do.

In a game at Philadelphia, Barry hit two homers and drove in a career-high six runs. At San Diego, he scored five runs in a game to tie a team record set 30 years earlier by Willie Mays. At Chicago, he hit back-to-back home runs with Matt Williams twice. Against Florida, he stole three bases. By late July, the Giants were in first place in the National League West by 10 games.

But the baseball season is long. There are plenty of opportunities to hit a cold streak. The Giants froze up in September. They lost eight straight games—all at home. The Atlanta Braves passed them in the standings. All of a sudden, the Braves were four games ahead with just two weeks left.

Barry had been in playoff races before. He would not let the Giants quit. In the final 16 games of the season, he almost single-handedly carried the team with six homers, seven doubles, 21 RBIs, and a slugging percentage of .660. The Giants and Braves battled it out down the stretch. They had the two best records in baseball.

The Giants were one game behind on the last day of the 1993 season when they met the Dodgers in Los Angeles. The game was scoreless until the third inning when the Dodgers broke through with two runs. They scored another run in the fourth, but the Giants answered with a run in the fifth inning to make it 3-1. Then the Dodgers exploded. Mike Piazza whacked a home run in the sixth, and then Piazza bombed a three-run homer in the eighth. The Dodgers scored five runs on their way to a 12-1 rout.

It was a crushing end to San Francisco's promising year. Barry had posted amazing numbers: .331 average, 46 home runs, 123 RBIs, 29 stolen bases. He was an easy choice again as the league's Most Valuable Player.

Barry brought his son, Nikolai, and his daughter, Shikari, to the ballpark.

Barry had also endeared himself to San Francisco fans by buying $10,000 worth of tickets and giving them to children during the summer months. He gave away 50 tickets for 42 games. Kids would sit in leftfield above the "Bonds Squad" sign. When he took the field in the first inning, Barry would look up to the stands and tip his cap to the children.

Still, Barry was not satisfied with his team's accomplishments. He yearned to play in the World Series. In 1994, he would miss out again. Barry was teamed with Matt Williams and Darryl Strawberry in the heart of the Giants' order. He was posting huge numbers again. With two months still to go in the season, Barry already had 37 home runs, 81 RBIs, and 29 stolen bases. The Giants were three games behind the Dodgers in the standings, but closing fast. Then it all stopped.

Baseball players and owners couldn't agree on salaries. The players went on strike. Barry was paid well, but he supported his teammates. The issue wasn't resolved, and the season came to a halt. For the first time since 1904, there was no World Series.

Barry was also having a bad time at home. He and Sun had decided to get a divorce. Although they would no longer live together, they agreed to share the care of their two children.

The 1995 season was much better for Barry. The Giants started slowly, but Barry brought them back with his power. In one six-game stretch in early July, he hit three game-winning home runs. First, Barry clubbed a three-run home run in the bottom of the ninth for a 7-6 victory over the San Diego Padres. Then, at Cincinnati, Barry hit a solo home run in the eighth inning for an 8-7 win over the Reds. He followed up the next night with a three-run blast in the ninth inning for a 7-5 victory. With a sweep of the Reds, the Giants moved into second place, three games behind the Colorado Rockies.

When Giants cleanup hitter Matt Williams suffered a broken foot, Barry tried to carry the offense by himself, but he couldn't do it. Opposing pitchers frustrated Barry by not giving him many good pitches to hit. Barry wound up leading the league with 120 walks. When Barry did hit the ball, he hit it with power. He finished with 33 home runs and 31 stolen bases. It was the third time he had achieved the 30-30 mark, and the first time a San Francisco Giant had accomplished the feat in 22 years. The last Giant to do it? Bobby Bonds.

The Giants finished the 1995 season in last place by 11 games, but Barry will get more chances to play in a World Series. He is one of only nine players who have won the MVP award three times. He expects to be the first to win it four times or more. "I've never let down in my confidence," he says, "because if you don't believe in yourself, no one else will."

Some people say Barry is too much of a showman. "It's like I become a Hollywood star on the field, like Michael Jackson," he says. "I can't dance like him or excite people like he does, but I can hit my glove on my chest and people like it because it's a move no one's seen before. When I jump over the wall for a ball, I feel like Michael Jordan flying in air. When I crash into the wall, I'm Rambo, this invincible man."

Barry says he has a recurring dream. Naturally, it's about baseball. He describes his dream this way: "I'm at the ballpark. I hit a home run and run the bases. Then I hit another one. I hit three. I hit four. Now I have a chance to hit five and break the all-time record. All of a sudden I'm at a zoo, or up on top of the Empire State Building, trying to get back to Shea Stadium to play the Mets. I can see they're trying to find me. But they go, 'Wait a minute, he's gone,' and they send up a pinch hitter."

Barry is full of confidence. That is why he dreams of hitting four home runs in a game. But every so often, fear creeps into his head. He feels the fear of not playing any more, the fear of being replaced by a pinch hitter, the fear of failure. Barry is motivated by both feelings—confidence and fear. He knows he can succeed. He also knows how much work it takes to be the best. He realized it one day in Fred Tate's barbershop. He has worked hard ever since to be the best.

Career Highlights

College Statistics

Year	Team	Games	At Bats	Runs	Hits	Home Runs	Runs Batted In	Stolen Bases	Batting Average
1983	Arizona State	64	206	60	63	11	54	16	.306
1984	Arizona State	70	258	62	93	11	55	30	.360
1985	Arizona State	62	247	61	91	23	66	11	.368
Totals		**196**	**711**	**183**	**247**	**45**	**175**	**57**	**.347**

Minor Leagues Statistics

Year	Team	Games	At Bats	Runs	Hits	Home Runs	Runs Batted In	Stolen Bases	Batting Average
1985	Prince William	71	254	49	76	13	37	15	.299
1986	Hawaii	44	148	30	46	7	37	16	.311

Major Leagues Statistics

Year	Team	Games	At Bats	Runs	Hits	Home Runs	Runs Batted In	Stolen Bases	Batting Average
1986	Pittsburgh	113	413	72	92	16	48	36	.223
1987	Pittsburgh	150	551	99	144	25	59	32	.261
1988	Pittsburgh	144	538	97	152	24	58	17	.283
1989	Pittsburgh	159	580	96	144	19	58	32	.248
1990	Pittsburgh	151	519	104	156	33	114	52	.301
1991	Pittsburgh	153	510	95	149	25	116	43	.292
1992	Pittsburgh	140	473	109	147	34	103	39	.311
1993	San Francisco	159	539	129	181	46	123	29	.336
1994	San Francisco	112	391	89	122	37	81	29	.312
1995	San Francisco	144	506	109	149	33	104	31	.294
Totals		**1,425**	**5,020**	**999**	**1,436**	**292**	**864**	**340**	**.286**

Honors

- Selected to the National League All-Star Team, 1990, 1991, 1992, 1993, 1994, 1995
- Gold Glove Award, 1990, 1991, 1992, 1993, 1994, 1995
- Silver Slugger Award, 1990, 1991, 1992, 1993, 1994, 1995
- Most Valuable Player in the National League, 1990, 1992, 1993

ABOUT THE AUTHOR

Jeff Savage was born in Oakland, California, and grew up in nearby Fremont. He graduated from the University of California at San Diego in 1988 with a degree in journalism and worked as a sportswriter for eight years at the San Diego Union-Tribune. He is the author of more than 30 books for young readers. In addition to his work as a writer, he also plays golf, practices karate, and flies airplanes. Jeff lives with his wife, Nancy, in Napa, California.

ACKNOWLEDGMENTS

Photographs are reproduced with the permission of: pp. 1, 38, 39, 57, 62, © ALL-SPORT USA/Otto Greule; p. 2, © John Klein; p. 6, © ALLSPORT USA/Jonathan Daniel; pp. 9, 10, 48, 50, 55, 58, 61, © Mickey Pfleger; pp. 12, 19, 20, 21, Serra High School; pp. 14, 17, 29, 44, UPI/Bettmann; pp. 15, 34, San Francisco Giants Archives; pp. 22, 24, Arizona State University, Sports Information, Chuck Conley Photo; p. 27, © ALLSPORT USA/Pensinger; pp. 30, 37, 42, 54, SportsChrome East/West; pp. 32, 45, SportsChrome East/West, Robert Tringali Jr.; p. 40, © ALLSPORT USA/Rick Stewart; p. 46, © ALLSPORT USA/Ken Levine; p. 51, Reuters/Bettmann; pp. 52, 53, San Francisco Giants/Martha Jane Stanton; p. 64, Jeff Savage.

Front cover photograph by SportsChrome East/West. Back cover photograph by © Mickey Pfleger.

Artwork by John Erste.